Dear MOTHER,   12-01

   THIS BOOK IS JUST A SMALL
EXPRESSION OF HOW MUCH I WILL
ALWAYS LOVE YOU. MAY IT BRING
YOU A SMILE EVERY TIME YOU
READ IT. FOR YOU ARE MY
CLOSEST FRIEND, MY MOTHER.

Presented to

_____

On the occasion of

_____

From

_____

Date

_____

ISBN 1-57748-986-1

Published by Barbour Publishing, Inc., P.O. Box 719, Uhrichsville, Ohio 44683
http://www.barbourbooks.com

Member of the
Evangelical Christian
Publishers Association

Printed in China.

MY MOTHER,
My Friend

A THANK-YOU NOTE
EXPRESSING MY LOVE

Written and compiled by
Sheryl Lynn Hill

BARBOUR
PUBLISHING, INC.

All I Am

My mother was the most beautiful woman I ever saw. All I am I owe to my mother. I attribute all my success in life to the moral, intellectual, and physical education I received from her.　　　　　GEORGE WASHINGTON

. . .

Whatever you do, work at it
with all your heart, as working for the Lord.

COLOSSIANS 3:23

She gets up while it is still dark...
and her lamp does not go out at night.

PROVERBS 31:15, 18

. . .

My sainted mother taught me a devotion to God and a love to country which have ever sustained me in my many lonely and bitter moments of decision in distant and hostile lands. To her, I yield anew a son's reverent thanks.   GENERAL DOUGLAS MACARTHUR

Heartfelt Thanks

- This is a thank-you note to mothers who didn't win the "Mother of the Year" award, even though they were deserving.

- This is for mothers who have persevered through heat and cold, rain and snow, as they sat on wooden benches, cheering for their children on the athletic field.

- This is for mothers who sat up all night with sick children, loving and rocking them and singing sweet melodies.

- This is for mothers who have been "taxi drivers" for their own children as well as all the kids in the neighborhood.

- This is for mothers who have spent endless hours reading to their children, especially that bedtime story "one more time."

- This is for mothers who have made mistakes and wished they could have done a better job.

- This is for mothers who labored teaching their children how to tie their shoes.

- This is for mothers who sat down and cried because their babies wouldn't stop crying.

- This is for mothers with bottles in their purses and spit-up stains on their clothes.

- This is for mothers who grieved as they lay flowers on a child's grave.

- This is for mothers who cried and prayed for wayward children when they ran away from home.

- This is for mothers who learned to let go.

Thank you, Mother!

Love and Sacrifice

Now that I have children of my own, I realize the love and sacrifice it takes to be a good mother.

Mother, you always made Christmas special with your beautifully decorated trees. I used to gaze in awe at the tree all lit up at night and shimmering with dazzling colors.

Mother, you frequently baked cookies and cakes, never putting a limit on what we could eat. And yes, you let me make messes in the kitchen as I tried to bake just like you.

Mother, you made sure we said our prayers at night, and that we knew who God was.

Mother, you made sure I had a beautiful prom dress and shoes. Once again, you made a sacrifice that I would not understand until I became a mother.

Thank you, Mother.

The successful mother, the mother who does her part in rearing and training aright the boys and girls who are to be the men and women of the next generation, is of greater use to the community. . . . She is more important by far than the successful statesman or businessman or artist or scientist.   THEODORE ROOSEVELT

· · ·

My mother said to me, "If you become a soldier you'll be a general; if you become a monk you'll end up as the pope." Instead, I became a painter and wound up as Picasso.   PABLO PICASSO

A Model of Strength

Mother, you are a woman of strength and honor. In spite of the childhood trauma that deprived you of having a loving model for parents, you have succeeded in being a loving and supportive mother to me.

You depended on God and raised me with faithful concern for my best interests, humbly asking my forgiveness for your failings. You have been a model of strength, stability, and support.

From your example, I learned to love unconditionally, value family, and focus on God. I'm so glad that God chose you as my mother and I love you very much. Thank you, Mother!

KATHY COLLARD MILLER

A mother is the truest friend we have, when trials, heavy and sudden, fall upon us; when adversity takes the place of prosperity; when friends who rejoice with us in our sunshine desert us when troubles thicken around us; still will she cling to us, and endeavor by her kind precepts and counsel to dissipate the clouds of darkness, and cause peace to return to our hearts.

WASHINGTON IRVING

She sets about her work vigorously;
her arms are strong for her tasks.
PROVERBS 31: 17

. . .

The awareness of our own strength makes us modest.

PAUL CEZANNE

. . .

She is clothed with strength and dignity.
PROVERBS 31:25

Mom, You're the Greatest

You are my chauffeur, ATM, and cook. On a more serious note, you're always there for me, even when I am a brat.

You're the shoulder I cry on, my mentor and confidante, and my one-person cheering squad.

You do my laundry when I am too busy. You make me tea when I am sick.

Sometimes you buy me things, as you go without. You put up with my money-eating horse and pay for my riding lessons.

Yet you never complain.

Mom, you're the greatest! Thank you.

JESSICA J. HILL

All that I am or hope to be I owe to my angel mother.
I remember my mother's prayers
and they have always followed me.
They have clung to me all my life.

ABRAHAM LINCOLN

. . .

I'd love to be a child again in mother's tender care;
she sang the sweetest lullaby and listened to my prayer.
Gentle Jesus, meek, and mild. . .
keep me ever close to Thee.

LILLIE OLSON BERGGREN

A Mother's Prayers

My mother prayed for me as I was growing up, and for several years my mother's faith was tested. Many times she didn't know where I was or what I was doing. The only thing she could do was pray.

Instead of fretting, my mother prayed and committed me into God's hands. She gained comfort knowing that God watched over me at all times and in every situation.

I am convinced that her prayers were answered concerning my life, as God surely guided me through my troubled teen years.

. . .

I prayed for this child,
and the LORD has granted me what I asked of him.
So now I give him to the LORD.

1 SAMUEL 1:27–28

Kind words are short and easy to speak,
but their echoes are truly endless.

MOTHER TERESA

. . .

Pleasant words are a honeycomb, sweet to the soul and
healing to the bones.   PROVERBS 16:24

The Special Card

When I was ten, my mother lovingly expressed to me how special it was to be a middle child. I had been feeling left out. My sisters and I had to share a bedroom and we were not getting along.

One morning when I woke up, I noticed a card beside my bed. My mother had written an acrostic of my name, with each letter beginning a word that described a special quality of mine.

Mother knew exactly what I needed, and for that I am grateful. Thank you, Mother.

If you laugh a lot, when you get older your wrinkles will be in the right places. AUTHOR UNKNOWN

. . .

Sarah said, "God has brought me laughter."

GENESIS 21:6

Medicine for the Heart

Several weeks before my mother died, she began losing a lot of weight and was unable to walk. One afternoon I wanted to make her a nice lunch. Although she insisted that she didn't want to eat anything substantial, I was determined to make her a nice sandwich.

My mother sat in the living room and watched me fixing her lunch in the kitchen.

As I turned around to look at her, our eyes met. Much to my surprise, we both stuck our tongues out at each other at the same time. We burst into laughter and laughed for several minutes.

Thank you, Mom. I will always treasure this memory.

GINA DEVILLE

To My Mother

Because I feel that in heaven above
The angels, whispering one to another,
Can find among their burning terms of love,
None so devotional as that of "Mother,"
Therefore by that dear name I have long called you,
You who are more than mother to me.

EDGAR ALLAN POE

The Simple Joys of Childhood

When I was a little girl of about five or six, we lived in a beautiful house by a river. There my mother read me Mother Goose rhymes until I could recite them by heart. At night she prayed with me the well-known prayer that begins, "Now I lay me down to sleep."

My mother often watched from the kitchen window as I played in the yard.

When I wanted to walk the short distance to visit the older couple I had "adopted" as my grandparents, I'd call out, "See you later, alligator!" Mother would laugh and reply, "After while, crocodile."

Today when life gets too stressful, I wish for those days of childhood. In my memories I soar back to the beautiful house by the river. It is summer, and I can hear my mother reading Mother Goose and feel her love and acceptance.

TAMERA TERRY

She Made My Home a Heaven

I am thankful because my mother taught me the meaning of unconditional love. As the youngest of four children, I could never do anything that would stop her from loving me.

No matter what, I could always come home.

My mother made our home a place of total love and acceptance. Even though there were times my mother trusted me when she shouldn't have, she gave me the benefit of the doubt, and her trust made me want to do better.

She was my friend as well as my cheerleader, always rooting for me. In high school I never felt pretty or popular, but at home she made me feel like a beautiful homecoming queen.

Now that I am grown with four kids of my own, I hope I can make my home a heaven, one full of unconditional love, as my mother did for me. Thank you, Mother.

VIRGINIA HEATHERTON

Her children arise and call her blessed;
her husband also, and he praises her. . . .
Give her the reward she has earned,
and let her works bring her praise at the city gate.

PROVERBS 31: 28, 31

. . .

I know that in creating the home in which I was raised,
my mother didn't do a perfect job due largely to the
less-than-perfect situation she had to work in and
the less-than-perfect material she had to work with.
But I also know that she did a great deal that was right,
and I am and shall remain eternally grateful to her and
for her.

JOHN R. DELLENBACK
from *What My Parents Did Right*

There is an enduring tenderness in the love of a mother to a son that transcends all other affections of the heart! It is neither to be chilled by selfishness, nor daunted by danger, nor weakened by worthlessness, nor stifled by ingratitude. She will sacrifice every comfort to his convenience; she will surrender every pleasure to his enjoyment; she will glory in his fame, and exult in his prosperity—and if misfortune overtake him he will be the dearer to her for misfortune; and if disgrace settle upon his name she will still love and cherish him in spite of his disgrace; and if all the world beside cast him off she will be all the world to him.

WASHINGTON IRVING

Stitched Together by Love

My mother always took care of herself. She was an attractive woman, but there was much more to her than looks. My mother was a woman of strong and noble character.

When I was a young boy, money was scarce but my mother never complained.

She always worked hard and took care of our farm in northern Minnesota. For ten years my mother also took loving care of her invalid mother, all by herself and without complaint.

As a teenager, I went through some turbulent and troubled years. Yet my mother was always there for me. She believed in and prayed for me. When everyone else gave up, my mother stood by me.

My mother's love kept me stitched together. Thank you, Mother.

DONALD BAXTER

Spiritual Mother

I have been blessed to know a woman I call my spiritual mother. At eighty-four years of age, she is still a beautiful woman, but more importantly, she has a beautiful spirit.

I met Mildred several years ago in church. The church had a "spiritual mother-daughter program" where the older women adopted younger women, based on Titus 2:3–5. Over the years we have built a strong mother-daughter relationship.

I can call her any time of the day or night and she will be there to listen to and encourage me. This has been a big help, as my husband's job often keeps him away from home for extended periods of time.

Even though we no longer live nearby each other, Mildred and I still keep in touch. I consider her my spiritual mother, and she considers me her daughter.

Thank you, Mother.

What Mother Taught

When I was a young girl, a major strike happened in our town, leaving my family unemployed. Soon we had no money and our utilities were shut off.

My mother, however, made this trial into an adventure. We sat around at night and made tiny dolls with the wax that dripped from the candles, all the while making up stories about the dolls' lives.

It was one of the best summers of my life. Thank you, Mother.

. . .

No man is poor who has a godly mother.

ABRAHAM LINCOLN

Pickles, Pearls, and Poor Adventure

Even though we were often poor as I was growing up, my mother taught us that we were rich in God's provisions.

On a favorite family outing, we would climb into the "Golden Nugget," our affectionate name for the family station wagon, and drive up the coast to Ports O' Call in San Pedro, California.

The Ports O' Call village, a tourist attraction, was always a special place for me. I loved to meander through the specialty shops, oohing and aahing at all the baubles from faraway places with strange-sounding names. The glassblowers especially mesmerized my mother. She and I would watch them work for hours. Then we'd stroll along the waterfront, taking in all the sights, sounds, and smells.

The Japanese pearl divers were particularly fascinating. Demure ladies in white bathing suits would dive into the ocean to retrieve oysters and bring them back to the surface, where we eagerly waited. We giggled with anticipation as they cut open the oysters to search for the hidden treasures. Would it be a black, blue, pink, cream-colored, or white pearl? Would there be one or two pearls inside the oyster?

On this particular day, as we headed back to the Golden Nugget, we were stopped in the parking lot by a man with a cart holding a large glass barrel full of dill pickles. A convincing salesman, he enticed us to spend our last two dollars. Mom let us pick out two of the biggest, juiciest pickles we had ever seen in our lives. As I clutched a pearl in one hand and a pickle in the other, my family dubbed this day our "Pickles, Pearls, and Poor Adventure."

Over a quarter of a century has passed since that wondrous day, and many years since my mother's death. I have been to that village a few times since then, but none of those visits compares with that day, one that remains alive because of the memories in my heart.

Thank you, Mother.

DEBBIE RAMOS

She speaks with wisdom,
and faithful instruction is on her tongue.

PROVERBS 31:26

. . .

Knowledge is the parent of love;
wisdom, love itself.

JULIUS CHARLES HARE
AUGUSTUS WILLIAM HARE

Mother's Directions

When my mother moved near my home in California, I had already lived in the area for several years. Consequently, whenever we went anywhere, I always drove. Knowing me as well as she did, my mother knew that when I was busy talking, I'd forget where I was going. As my mother became familiar with the area, she told me where to turn and when to stop.

Once my sister-in-law was in the car with us. Suddenly she started laughing. When I asked her what was so funny, she replied, "Listening to you two. Since I got into this car, your mom has told you every move to make, and you just do it."

Usually I hate when people tell me what to do. But with my mother, I never even noticed. Thank you, Mother.

JANE FOSTER

*But we were gentle among you,
like a mother caring for her little children.*

1 THESSALONIANS 2:7

. . .

A mother's arms are made of tenderness
and children sleep soundly in them.
VICTOR HUGO

Arms of Love

When I was a child my dad would get up early to milk the cows. After I heard him leave, I'd get out of my bed and go climb in with Mom. She would wrap her arms around me and hold me close. This made me feel so comforted and loved. Thank you, Mother.

NANCY SANDERS

. . .

He tends his flock like a shepherd:
He gathers the lambs in his arms
and carries them close to his heart;
he gently leads those that have young.

ISAIAH 40:11

Best Friend

My mother had problems that made it hard for me to have a close relationship with her.

Many times I had to be the mother to her, and often I was angry at her for taking away my childhood. When we had no contact with each other for a year, I thought there was no hope for our relationship. But God had another plan.

Suddenly, my mom contacted me and wanted to start over. I was a bit skeptical, but I had been praying for this and I wasn't about to ignore God's answer.

Soon after that, I started college, which was close to my mother's apartment. She began visiting me during the week and then we started seeing each other on the weekends. We prayed together and shared our thoughts, hopes, and dreams.

My mother has now become my best friend. Thank you, Mother.

NICHOLE THONEY

Of all the rights of a woman,
the greatest is to be a mother.

LIN YUTANG

. . .

The mother's heart is the child's classroom.
HENRY WARD BEECHER

The Book of Life

All weekend long I had waited and hoped for this moment. My daughter, who was experiencing a personal crisis, and I had made a bittersweet pilgrimage to visit my elderly mother in the next state. For several days we visited various family members who offered love and encouragement. All along, I could tell Mother was waiting for just the right moment to talk to her beloved granddaughter.

Now our suitcases were packed for the trip home. As I made one final check of the bedroom, I heard Mother's walker in the adjoining room squeaking as she moved toward where my daughter stood. I heard their quiet words of affection, and then silence while I imagined they hugged one another. Mother's voice was strong as she spoke. I listened, spellbound.

"Oh, darling! I would give anything if this had not happened to you. I know how you feel because tragedy touched my life as well. Every morning when I rose, I thanked God for keeping me through the night and asked Him to guide me each day. When the day was done, I laid down to sleep as I prayed and thanked God again. Then I turned the page. You, too, must go on as your whole life is before you."

Then I heard quiet tears, and the sound of Mother's walker as they made their way to join me at the front door.

Even though it was too early for any real healing to begin, it was just the right time for a grandmother to have reached across the generations to offer the only solace she could give. She had suffered a similar loss; she understood something that many of us could not.

I have thought of my mother's wise testimony hundreds of times since that day. It has helped me through other dark valleys and long nights. When I lay my head down at night, I hear her voice saying, "And then I turned the page." Following her wise example, I take the book of my life and look toward the new day. Thank you, Mother.

KATHLEEN LEWIS

I have been reminded of your sincere faith,
which first lived in your grandmother Lois
and in your mother Eunice and,
I am persuaded, now lives in you also.

2 TIMOTHY 1:5

A mother had a slender, small body, but a large heart. . .a heart so large that everybody's grief and everybody's joy found welcome in it, and hospitable accommodation.

MARK TWAIN

. . .

It is more blessed to give than to receive.

ACTS 20:35

There are only two lasting bequests
we can hope to give our children.
One is roots; and the other, wings.

HODDING CARTER

. . .

Like kites without strings and butterfly wings,
my mother taught me to soar with my dreams.

WILLIAM H. MCMURRY III